Table of Contents

What is cyber security?

Cyber security is the practice of defending computers, servers, mobile devices, electronic systems, networks, and data from malicious attacks. It's also known as information technology security or electronic information security. The term applies in a variety of contexts, from business to mobile computing, and can be divided into a few common categories. Cyber security refers to the body of technologies, processes, and practices designed to protect networks, devices, programs, and data from attack, damage, or unauthorized access. Cyber security may also be referred to as information technology security. Cyber security protects the integrity of a computer's internet connected systems, hardware, software and data from cyber attacks. Without a security plan in place hackers can access your computer system and misuse your personal information, your customer's information, your business intel and much more.It seems that everything now relies on internet and computers entertainment, communication, transportation, medicine, shopping, etc. Even banking institutions run their business online. Cyber security has never been simple. And because attacks evolve every day as attackers become more inventive, it is critical to properly define cyber security and identify what constitutes good cyber security.

Why is this so important? Because year over year, the worldwide spend for cyber security continues to grow. Organizations are starting to understand that malware is a publicly available commodity that makes it easy for anyone to become a cyber attacker, and even more companies offer security solutions that do little to defend against attacks. Cyber security demands focus and dedication.

Cyber security protects the data and integrity of computing assets belonging to or connecting to an organization's network. Its purpose is to defend those assets against all threat actors throughout the entire life cycle of a cyber attack. It is the practice of defending computers, networks, and data from malicious electronic attacks. It is often contrasted with physical security, which is the more traditional security practice aimed at controlling access to buildings and other objects in the real world. Although there are plenty of high-tech physical security techni ues, and sometimes physical and cyber security are joined together in the org chart under the same executive, cyber security focuses on protecting assets from malicious logins and code, not burglaries.

Types of cyber security

· Network security is the practice of securing a computer network from intruders, whether targeted attackers or opportunistic malware. As cyber security is concerned with outside threats, network security guards against unauthorized intrusion of your internal networks due to malicious intent. Network security ensures that internal networks are secure by protecting the infrastructure and inhibiting access to it.

To help better manage network security monitoring, security teams are now using machine learning to flag abnormal traffic and alert to threats in real time. Network administrators continue to implement policies and procedures to prevent unauthorized access, modification and exploitation of the network.

Common examples of network security implementation:

- extra logins
- new passwords
- application security
- antivirus programs
- antispyware software
- encryption
- firewalls
- Monitored internet access

· Application security focuses on keeping software and devices free of threats. A compromised application could provide access to the data its designed to protect. Successful security begins in the design stage, well before a program or device is deployed. You should choose application security as one of the several must-have security measures adopted to protect your systems. Application security uses software and hardware methods to tackle external threats that can arise in the development stage of an application.

Applications are much more accessible over networks, causing the adoption of security measures during the development phase to be an imperative phase of the project.

Types of application security:

- antivirus programs

- firewalls
- encryption programs

These help to ensure that unauthorized access is prevented. Companies can also detect sensitive data assets and protect them through specific application security processes attached to these data sets.

· Information security protects the integrity and privacy of data, both in storage and in transit. Information security aims to protect the users' private information from unauthorized access, identity theft. It protects the privacy of data and hardware that handle, store and transmit that data. Examples of Information security include User Authentication and Cryptography. Information Security is not only about securing information from unauthorized access. Information Security is basically the practice of preventing unauthorized access, use, disclosure, disruption, modification, inspection, recording or destruction of information. Information can be physical or electronic one. Information can be anything like Your details or we can say your profile on social media, your data in mobile phone, your biometrics etc. sometimes also referred to as data security, keeps data secure from unauthorized access or alterations, both when it's being stored and when it's being transmitted from one machine to another

· Operational security includes the processes and decisions for handling and protecting data assets. The permissions users have when accessing a network and the procedures that determine how and where data may be stored or shared all fall under this umbrella. Operations security is a process that identifies friendly actions that could be useful for a potential attacker if properly analyzed and grouped with other data to reveal critical information or sensitive data. OPSEC uses countermeasures to reduce or eliminate adversary exploitation.

OPSEC is both an analytical process and a strategy used in risk management to identify information that can be exploited by an attacker and used to collect critical information that could damage an organization's plans or reputation.

· Disaster recovery and business continuity define how an organization responds to a cyber-security incident or any other event that causes the loss of operations or data. Disaster recovery policies dictate how the organization restores its operations and information to return to the same operating capacity as before the event. Business continuity is the plan the organization falls back on while trying to operate without certain resources. DR&BC deals with processes, monitoring, alerts and plans that help organizations prepare for keeping business critical systems online during and after any kind of a disaster as well as resuming lost operations and systems after an incident. Disaster recovery planning is a process that includes performing risk assessment, establishing priorities, developing recovery strategies in case of a disaster. Any business should have a concrete plan for disaster recovery to resume normal business operations as quickly as possible after a disaster.

· End-user education addresses the most unpredictable cyber-security factor: people. Anyone can accidentally introduce a virus to an otherwise secure system by failing to follow good security practices. Teaching users to delete suspicious email attachments, not plug in unidentified USB drives, and various other important lessons is vital for the security of any organization. A good end-user security training program is an inexpensive way to enhance your security in your organization, but it must be done properly. The information has to be given in a language and at a technical level that everyone can understand. Security Awareness programs enable organizations to improve their security posture by giving employees the knowledge and understanding they need to better protect valuable security information assets through proactive, security-conscious behavior.

Security Awareness programs can be designed to help companies meet regulatory requirements, reduce vulnerabilities by creating a more security aware workforce, increase security knowledge and understanding, and influence appropriate employee behavior at all levels of the workforce

THE IMPORTANCE OF CYBER SECURITY

Cyber security is important because government, military, corporate, financial, and medical organizations collect, process, and store unprecedented amounts of data on computers and other devices. A significant portion of that data can be sensitive information, whether that be intellectual property, financial data, personal information, or other types of data for which unauthorized access or exposure could have negative consequences. Organizations transmit sensitive data across networks and to other devices in the course of doing businesses, and cyber security describes the discipline dedicated to protecting that information and the systems used to process or store it. As the volume and sophistication of cyber attacks grow, companies and organizations, especially those that are tasked with safeguarding information relating to national security, health, or financial records, need to take steps to protect their sensitive business and personnel information. As early as March 2013, the nation's top intelligence officials cautioned that cyber attacks and digital spying are the top threat to national security, eclipsing even terrorism. With an increasing number of users, devices and programs in the modern enterprise, combined with the increased deluge of data much of which is sensitive or confidential the importance of cybersecurity continues to grow. The growing volume and sophistication of cyber attackers and attack techniques compound the problem even further.

The benefits of implementing and maintaining cybersecurity practices include:

- Business protection against cyberattacks and data breaches.
- Protection for data and networks.
- Prevention of unauthorized user access.
- Improved recovery time after a breach.
- Protection for end users and endpoint devices.
- Regulatory compliance.
- Business continuity.
- Improved confidence in the company's reputation and trust for developers, partners, customers, stakeholders and employees.

What is cyber attack?

A cyber-attack is a deliberate attempt by external or internal threats or attackers to exploit and compromise the confidentiality, integrity and availability of information systems of a target organization or individual(s). Cyber-attackers use illegal methods, tools and approaches to cause damages and disruptions or gain unauthorized access to computers, devices, networks, applications and databases.

Causes of Cybersecurity Threats

There are many different ways by which cyberthreats infects a victim's computer, some of the most common ways are listed below.

Shady Websites

Hackers use seemingly legitimate software and websites to lure users into downloading malware. The lure of free of free money or games entices some users. Even people who do not visit these shady sites are prone to enticing links being hidden on their computers.

Malware that originates from these sites may travel around the internet and land on an innocent users computer redirecting their browsing experience to these sites.

Peer to Peer File Sharing

Peer to Peer (P2P) file-sharing networks is one of the most popular ways to share movies, games, music, and other files online. In a typical P2P network, participants make a portion of their own computing resources available to other network participants.

In essence, file sharing over a P2P network allows computer users to share files directly from the computers of each other. P2P file sharing is also a very commonly used method for distributing malware and performing other malicious deeds.

Torrent Downloads and Phishing Emails

Trying to find a particular movie that is still in theaters? Maybe you want a free copy of the latest PC Game. Torrent sites are used by computer savvy users that have malware removal in their daily agenda.

Keygens, Cracks, Serial Coders, all of these might be what you need but don't be surprised when you are infected. In most cases, the file you are downloading could be a rogue malware installer written by a savvy programmer.

Email is the breeding ground for many malware. If you open a phishing email that is sent with an attachment, it instantly collects information within your email, mainly your address book. It will immediately send similar phishing emails to all of the contacts in your address book, spreading the problem.

MANAGING CYBER SECURITY

The National Cyber Security Alliance, through SafeOnline.org, recommends a top-down approach to cyber security in which corporate management leads the charge in prioritizing cyber security management across all business practices. NCSA advises that companies must be prepared to "respond to the inevitable cyber incident, restore normal operations, and ensure that company assets and the company's reputation are protected." NCSA's guidelines for conducting cyber risk assessments focus on three key areas: identifying your organization's "crown jewels," or your most valuable information requiring protection; identifying the threats and risks facing that information; and outlining the damage your organization would incur should that data be lost or wrongfully exposed. Cyber risk assessments should also consider any regulations that impact the way your company collects, stores, and secures data, such as PCI-DSS, HIPAA, SOX, FISMA, and others. Following a cyber risk assessment, develop and implement a plan to mitigate cyber risk, protect the "crown jewels" outlined in your assessment, and effectively detect and respond to security incidents. This plan should encompass both the processes and technologies required to build a mature cyber security program. An ever-evolving field, cyber security best practices must evolve to accommodate the increasingly sophisticated attacks carried out by attackers. Combining sound cyber security measures with an educated and security-minded employee base provides the best defense against cyber criminals attempting to gain access to your company's sensitive data. While it may seem like a daunting task, start small and focus on your most sensitive data, scaling your efforts as your cyber program matures.

Cyber security best practices to prevent a breach

1. Conduct cyber security training and awareness

A strong cyber security strategy would not be successful if the employees are not educated on topics of cyber security, company policies and incidence reporting. Even the best technical defenses may fall apart when employees make unintentional or intentional malicious actions resulting in a costly security breach. Educating employees and raising awareness of company policies and security best practices through seminars, classes, online courses is the best way to reduce negligence and the potential of a security violation.

2. Perform risk assessments

Organizations should perform a formal risk assessment to identify all valuable assets and prioritize them based on the impact caused by an asset when its compromised. This will help organizations decide how to best spend their resources on securing each valuable asset.

3. Ensure vulnerability management and software patch management/updates

It is crucial for organizational IT teams to perform identification, classification, remediation, and mitigation of vulnerabilities within all software and networks that it uses, to reduce threats against their IT systems. Furthermore, security researchers and attackers identify new vulnerabilities within various software every now and then which are reported back to the software vendors or released to the public. These vulnerabilities are often exploited by malware and cyber attackers. Software vendors periodically release updates which patch and mitigate these vulnerabilities. Therefore, keeping IT systems up-to-date helps protect organizational assets.

4. Use the principle of least privilege

The principle of least privilege dictates that both software and personnel should be allotted the least amount of permissions necessary to perform their duties. This helps limits the damage of a successful security breach as user accounts/software having lower permissions would not be able to impact valuable assets that require a higher-level set of permissions. Also, two-factor authentication should be used for all high-level user accounts that have unrestricted permissions.

5. Enforce secure password storage and policies

Organizations should enforce the use of strong passwords that adhere to industry recommended standards for all employees. They should also be forced to be periodically changed to help protect from compromised passwords. Furthermore, password storage should follow industry best practices of using salts and strong hashing algorithms.

6. Implement a robust business continuity and incidence response(BC-IR) plan

Having a solid BC-IR plans and policies in place will help an organization effectively respond to cyber-attacks and security breaches while ensuring critical business systems remain online.

7. Perform periodic security reviews

Having all software and networks go through periodic security reviews helps in identifying security issues early on and in a safe environment. Security reviews include application and network penetration testing, source code reviews, architecture design reviews, red team assessments, etc. Once security vulnerabilities are found, organizations should prioritize and mitigate them as soon as possible.

8. Backup data

Backing up all data periodically will increase redundancy and will make sure all sensitive data is not lost or comprised after a security breach. Attacks such as injections and ransomware, compromise the integrity and availability of data. Backups can help protect in such cases.

9. Use encryption for data at rest and in transit

All sensitive information should be stored and transferred using strong encryption algorithms. Encrypting data ensures confidentiality. Effective key management and rotation policies should also be put in place. All web applications/software should employ the use of SSL/TLS.

10. Design software and networks with security in mind

When creating applications, writing software, architecting networks, always design them with security in place. Bear in mind that the cost of refactoring software and adding security measures later on is far greater than building in security from the start. Security designed application help reduce the threats and ensure that when software/networks fail, they fail safe.

11. Implement strong input validation and industry standards in secure coding

Strong input validation is often the first line of defense against various types of injection attacks. Software and applications are designed to accept user input which opens it up to attacks and here is where strong input validation helps filter out malicious input payloads that the application would process. Furthermore, secure coding standards should be used when writing software as these helps avoid most of the prevalent vulnerabilities outlined in OWASP and CVE.

Some common methods used to threaten cyber-security

Malware

Malware means malicious software. One of the most common cyber threats, malware is software that a cybercriminal or hacker has created to disrupt or damage a legitimate user's computer. Often spread via an unsolicited email attachment or legitimate-looking download, malware may be used by cybercriminals to make money or in politically motivated cyber-attacks.

There are a number of different types of malware, including:

- Virus: A self-replicating program that attaches itself to clean file and spreads throughout a computer system, infecting files with malicious code.
- Trojans: A type of malware that is disguised as legitimate software. Cybercriminals trick users into uploading Trojans onto their computer where they cause damage or collect data.

- Spyware: A program that secretly records what a user does, so that cybercriminals can make use of this information. For example, spyware could capture credit card details.
- Ransomware: Malware which locks down a user's files and data, with the threat of erasing it unless a ransom is paid.
- Adware: Advertising software which can be used to spread malware.
- Botnets: Networks of malware infected computers which cybercriminals use to perform tasks online without the user's permission.

Malware is used to describe malicious software, including spyware, ransomware and viruses. It usually breaches networks through a vulnerability, like clicking on suspicious email links or installing a risky application. Once inside a network, malware can obtain sensitive information, further produce more harmful software throughout the system and can even block access to vital business network components (ransomware).

SQL injection

An SQL (structured language query) injection is a type of cyber-attack used to take control of and steal data from a database. Cybercriminals exploit vulnerabilities in data-driven applications to insert malicious code into a databased via a malicious SQL statement. This gives them access to the sensitive information contained in the database. SQL injection has become a common issue with database-driven websites. It occurs when a malefactor executes a SQL query to the database via the input data from the client to server. SQL commands are inserted into data-plane input (for example, instead of the login or password) in order to run predefined SQL commands. A successful SQL injection exploit can read sensitive data from the database, modify (insert, update or delete) database data, execute administration operations (such as shutdown) on the database, recover the content of a given file, and, in some cases, issue commands to the operating system.

Phishing

Phishing is when cybercriminals target victims with emails that appear to be from a legitimate company asking for sensitive information. Phishing attacks are often used to dupe people into handing over credit card data and other personal information. Phishing is the practice of sending malicious communications (usually emails) designed to appear from reputable, well-known sources. These emails use the same names, logos, wording, etc., as a CEO or company to dull suspicions and get victims to click on harmful links. Once a phishing link is clicked, cyber criminals have access to sensitive data like credit card, social security or login information.

Man-in-the-middle attack

A man-in-the-middle attack is a type of cyber threat where a cybercriminal intercepts communication between two individuals in order to steal data. For example, on an unsecure WiFi network, an attacker could intercept data being passed from the victim's device and the network. Man-in-the-Middle (MitM) attacks occur when criminals interrupt the traffic between a two-party transaction. For example, criminals can insert themselves between a public Wi-Fi and an individual's device. Without a protected Wi-Fi connection, cyber criminals can sometimes view all of a victim's information without ever being caught.

Denial-of-service attack

A denial-of-service attack is where cybercriminals prevent a computer system from fulfilling legitimate re uests by overwhelming the networks and servers with traffic. This renders the system unusable, preventing an organization from carrying out vital functions. A denial-of-service attack overwhelms a system's resources so that it cannot respond to service requests. A DDoS attack is also an attack on system's resources, but it is launched from a large number of other host machines that are infected by malicious software controlled by the attacker.

Unlike attacks that are designed to enable the attacker to gain or increase access, denial-of-service doesn't provide direct benefits for attackers. For some of them, it's enough to have the satisfaction of service denial. However, if the attacked resource belongs to a business competitor, then the benefit to the attacker may be real enough. Another purpose of a DoS attack can be to take a system offline so that a different kind of attack can be launched.

Zero-day attack

Zero-day attacks are becoming more-and-more common. Essentially, these attacks occur between a network vulnerability announcement and a patch solution. In the name of transparency and security, most companies will announce that they found a problem with their network safety, but some criminals will take this opportunity to unleash attacks before the company can come up with a security patch.

Social Engineering

Social engineering is the process of psychologically manipulating people into divulging personal information. Phishing is a form of social engineering, where criminals take advantage of people's natural curiosity or trust. An example of more advanced social engineering is with voice manipulation. In this case, cyber criminals take an individual's voice (from sources like a voicemail or social media post) and manipulate it to call friends or relatives and ask for credit card or other personal information.

Eavesdropping attack

Eavesdropping attacks occur through the interception of network traffic. By eavesdropping, an attacker can obtain passwords, credit card numbers and other confidential information that a user might be sending over the network. Eavesdropping can be passive or active:

- Passive eavesdropping — A hacker detects the information by listening to the message transmission in the network.

- Active eavesdropping — A hacker actively grabs the information by disguising himself as friendly unit and by sending queries to transmitters. This is called probing, scanning or tampering.

Cybersecurity Basics

A multi-layer cybersecurity approach is the best way to thwart any serious cyber attack. A combination of firewalls, software and a variety of tools will help combat malware that can affect everything from mobile phones to Wi-Fi. Here are some of the ways cybersecurity experts fight the onslaught of digital attacks.

AI FOR CYBERSECURITY

AI is being used in cybersecurity to thwart a wide variety of malicious cybercrimes. Security companies are training artificial intelligence tools to predict data breaches, alert to phishing attempts in real-time and even expose social engineering scams before they become dangerous.

Securing Against Malware

Security against malware is certainly one of the most important issues today (and it will continue to be as malicious software evolves). An anti-virus software package is needed to combat any suspicious activity. These packages usually include tools that do everything from warning against suspicious websites to flagging potentially harmful emails.

Mobile Security

Mobile phones are one of the most at-risk devices for cyber attacks and the threat is only growing. Device loss is the top concern among cybersecurity experts. Leaving our phones at a restaurant or in the back of a rideshare can prove dangerous. Luckily, there are tools that lock all use of mobile phones (or enact multi-factor passwords) if this incident occurs. Application security is also becoming another major issue. To combat mobile apps that re uest too many privileges, introduce Trojan viruses or leak personal information, experts turn to cybersecurity tools that will alert or altogether block suspicious activity.

Web Browser Security & the Cloud

Browser security is the application of protecting internet-connected, networked data from privacy breaches or malware. Anti-virus browser tools include pop-up blockers, which simply alert or block spammy, suspicious links and advertisements. More advanced tactics include two-factor authentication, using security-focused browser plug-ins and using encrypted browsers.

Wi-Fi Security

Using public Wi-Fi can leave you vulnerable to a variety of man-in-the-middle cyber attacks. To secure against these attacks, most cybersecurity experts suggest using the most up-to-date software and to avoid password-protected sites that contain personal information (banking, social media, email, etc.). Arguably, the most secure way to guard against a cyber attack on public Wi-Fi is to use a virtual private network (VPN). VPNs create a secure network, where all data sent over a Wi-Fi connection is encrypted.

How is automation used in cybersecurity?

Automation has become an integral component to keep companies protected from the growing number and sophistication of cyberthreats. Using artificial intelligence (AI) and machine learning in areas with high-volume data streams can help improve cybersecurity in three main categories:

- Threat detection. AI platforms can analyze data and recognize known threats, as well as predict novel threats.
- Threat response. AI platforms also create and automatically enact security protections.
- Human augmentation. Security pros are often overloaded with alerts and repetitive tasks. AI can help eliminate alert fatigue by automatically triaging low-risk alarms and automating big data analysis and other repetitive tasks, freeing humans for more sophisticated tasks.

Other benefits of automation in cybersecurity include attack classification, malware classification, traffic analysis, compliance analysis and more.

Cybersecurity vendors and tools

Vendors in the cybersecurity field typically offer a variety of security products and services. Common security tools and systems include:

- Identity and access management (IAM)
- Firewalls
- Endpoint protection
- Antimalware
- Intrusion prevention/detection systems (IPS/IDS)
- Data loss prevention (DLP)
- Endpoint detection and response

- Security information and event management (SIEM)
- Encryption tools
- Vulnerability scanners
- Virtual private networks (VPNs)
- Cloud workload protection platform (CWPP)
- Cloud access security broker (CASB)

Well-known cybersecurity vendors include Check Point, Cisco, Code42, CrowdStrike, FireEye, Fortinet, IBM, Imperva, KnowBe4, McAfee, Microsoft, Palo Alto Networks, Rapid7, Splunk, Symantec, Trend Micro and Trustwave.

What are the career opportunities in cybersecurity?

As the cyberthreat landscape continues to grow and new threats emerge such as lot threats individuals are needed with cybersecurity awareness and hardware and software skills.

IT professionals and other computer specialists are needed in security roles, such as:

- Chief information security officer (CISO) is the individual who implements the security program across the organization and oversees the IT security department's operations.

- Chief security office (CSO) is the executive responsible for the physical and/or cybersecurity of a company.
- Security engineers protect company assets from threats with a focus on quality control within the IT infrastructure.
- Security architects are responsible for planning, analyzing, designing, testing, maintaining and supporting an enterprise's critical infrastructure.
- Security analysts have several responsibilities that include planning security measures and controls, protecting digital files, and conducting both internal and external security audits.
- Penetration testers are ethical hackers who test the security of systems, networks and applications, seeking

vulnerabilities that could be exploited by malicious actors.

- Threat hunters are threat analysts who aim to uncover vulnerabilities and attacks and mitigate them before they compromise a business.

Other cybersecurity careers include security consultants, data protection officer, cloud security architects, security operations manager (SOC) managers and analysts, security investigators, cryptographers and security administrators.

Skills Required for Cybersecurity Jobs

Problem-Solving Skills

As a cybersecurity professional, problem-solving will play a major role in your day to day work. Those in the field need to find creative ways to take on and address complex information security challenges across a variety of existing and emerging technologies and digital environments.

Technical Aptitude

As the name implies, cybersecurity is a technology-focused field: you will be likely be tasked with responsibilities such as troubleshooting, maintaining, and updating information security systems; implementing continuous network monitoring; and providing real-time security solutions. Being technologically savvy is essential in order to perform the daily activities of a cybersecurity professional.

Knowledge of Security Across Various Platforms

Cybersecurity isn't just limited to computers: you'll need to be comfortable working on a variety of operating systems, computer systems, mobile devices, cloud networks, and wireless networks and keep up to date on advances in the field for all of them.

Attention to Detail

Being able to defend an organization against cyber breaches requires you to be highly vigilant and detail oriented, in order to effectively detect vulnerabilities and risks. You'll like be responsible for continuous network monitoring and will need to be able to quickly identify concerns and come up with real time security solutions to address them.

Communication Skills

As a cybersecurity specialist, you'll be working closely with individuals in other roles and departments, and it's important to be able to effectively communicate and explain your findings, concerns, and solutions to others. It's important to be able to speak clearly and concisely on cybersecurity strategy and policy, as well as to be able to convey technical information to individuals of different levels of technical comprehension.

Fundamental Computer Forensics Skills

While computer forensics and cybersecurity are two separate fields, they're closely related - and having a foundation in computer forensics can help you excel in your cybersecurity career. To be able to effectively protect organizations' digital assets and prevent security breaches, you'll need to have a solid understanding of what happens if your efforts fail, and how compromised data is recovered. Most cybersecurity degree programs will have a computer forensics component for this reason.

A Desire to Learn

As with any technical field, cybersecurity is fast-changing. Anyone who works in the field will need to be committed to keeping current with best practices and emerging industry trends, and will always need to be learning and self-educating both on and off the clock.

An Understanding of Hacking

To effectively protect an organization's network and infrastructure, you'll need to know how they can be exploited in the first place that's why most cybersecurity professionals must learn how to "ethically hack." Essentially, you need to have the same skills as a hacker, to fully understand how a system could be breached, and in turn, create effective solutions for thwarting these attacks.

How Do You Build Cybersecurity Skills?

While some of the skills listed above are ones you should naturally have - for example, an inclination for analytical thinking and technology others are ones you will need to develop through formal training or education. Depending on your background, a certificate or degree in cybersecurity is a good place to start: they'll give you a solid foundation in the principles of cybersecurity, in addition to an overview of security across a variety of platforms, programming and development, digital forensic investigation, specific technical skills (such as those relating to computer and operating systems and networking) and more.

Given the growing popularity of this field, there are an increasing number of cybersecurity degree programs available to prospective students, both online and campus based. Regardless of the mode of learning you prefer, you should look for a school that is regionally accredited, non-profit, and has a well recognized cybersecurity program. Third-party validation from both the higher education industry (for example, U.S. News & World Report rankings) and the cybersecurity industry (such as SC Magazine's rankings) are important. And if possible, look for a program that has been recognized by the U.S. government for example, Champlain College has been designated a Center of Academic Excellence by the National

Security Administration and the Department of Homeland Security.